A CHILD'S COMFORT

A CHILD'S COMFORT
Baby and Doll Quilts in American Folk Art

Bruce Johnson

in collaboration with
Susan S. Connor, Josephine Rogers, and Holly Sidford

Harcourt Brace Jovanovich New York and London
in association with the Museum of American Folk Art

Library of Congress Cataloging in Publication Data

Johnson, Bruce, 1948–1976.
  A child's comfort.

  Catalogue of an exhibition held Oct. 5, 1976, through Jan. 23, 1977, at the Museum of American Folk Art, New York.
  1. Children's coverlets—United States—Exhibitions. 2. Doll coverlets—United States—Exhibitions. 3. Quilting. I. Museum of American Folk Art. II. Title.
NK9112.J63   746.9'7   76-27407
ISBN 0-15-117184-X

First edition

Photography by Terry McGinniss

Line drawings by Gary Tong

Designed by Ellen Louise Blissman

To Bruce Johnson

It was in the winter of 1975 that Bruce Johnson and I first discussed plans for *A Child's Comfort: Baby and Doll Quilts.* I had not looked at many baby or doll quilts, but as time went on and I began really seeing, my interest and love for children's quilts began to grow.

Bruce's interest was from the folk art point of view; mine was one of pattern design, color and fabric. We both had a great concern for the quality of workmanship in each quilt. Fortunately, Bruce and I finished our final selection the day before his death; this show is truly a representation of our joint efforts.

I should like to share with you some of the joy Bruce and I experienced while selecting these quilts, and I hope that viewing them gives you an understanding and feeling for the richness of the art and the painstaking effort necessary for their creation. This exhibition is dedicated to Bruce Johnson—his idea and his memory —which make this show a reality.

Josephine Rogers
Guest Curator

CONTENTS

1. DRUNKARD'S PATH
c. 1850–60
39″ × 43″
Indigo blue calico print and white cotton with these colors repeated in sawtooth border.
Collection of George E. Schoellkopf Gallery

ACKNOWLEDGMENTS

I wish to express my thanks:

To Mrs. R. R. Benson, who throughout the years has encouraged me in both my inner and outer life.

To Howard Lanser and Joe D'Agostino who have shown a great deal of kindness and concern, both with the help they have given toward the environment in the Museum, and with their advice on the display of the quilts. Their great knowledge in the field has helped to bring out the intrinsic beauty of each quilt on display.

To Barbara Nolan, my dear and devoted friend, who has helped unstintingly in my various quilting, teaching and community projects over the years. A special note of thank you to Barbara for her help with, and typing of, the original manuscript of this book.

To Barbara Okin, my student and friend, who always inspires me toward higher creative ideals.

To Karen S. Schuster, appointed administrator of the Museum of American Folk Art after Bruce Johnson's death. Without Karen's understanding and support this book and exhibition might not have been possible.

To David Weiss, who from my first quilting bee on the Great Lawn in Central Park has been a help and source of inspiration with many of my quilting projects.

Josephine Rogers
Guest Curator

2. DOUBLE PYRAMID DESIGN
c. 1850
65″ × 56″
White pieced cotton star with insets of red triangles to form sixteen circular designs on a white quilted background.
Collection of Shelburne Museum, Inc.

We wish to express our sincere gratitude to all those individuals who with their continued support and reassurance helped to complete this work. Special mention should be given Ellen Blissman, Nancy Druckman, Ralph Esmerian, Myron and Patsy Orlofsky, and Connie Schrader.

The following individuals, institutions and galleries generously made their pieces available for the exhibition: America Hurrah Antiques, Bedford Historical Society, Chase Manhattan Bank, David L. Davies, Christophe DeMenil, Tony Ellis and Bill Gallick, Molly Epstein, Mr. and Mrs. Morris Firtell, Phyllis Haders, Bryce and Donna Hamilton, Jonathan Holstein, Barbara S. Janos and Barbara Ross, Gloria List Antiques, Susan Grant Lewin and Harold Lewin, Richard and Rosemarie Machmer, Mr. and Mrs. Frank J. Miele, The Newark Museum, Esther and Christopher Pullman, Joanna S. Rose, George E. Schoellkopf Gallery, Robert Shallow, The Shelburne Museum, Marcia and Ron Spark, Thos. K. Woodard: American Antiques and Quilts, and Professor Matthew Wysocki. We thank them and the private collectors.

Karen S. Schuster
Museum of American Folk Art

PART I:

Child Life in the Nineteenth Century

Susan S. Connor and Holly Sidford

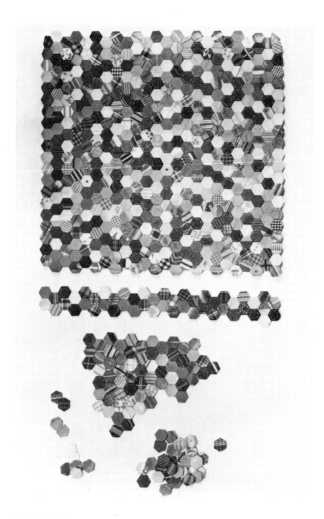

3. MOSAIC
   c. 1860
   13½″ × 13½″
   Pieced square of hexagonal pieces of multicolored silks sewn over
   paper patterns, plus one strip of same pattern and a box of 212
   hexagonal pieces .
   Collection of the Newark Museum

INTRODUCTION

Inanimate objects do gather into themselves something of the character of those who live among them, through association, and this alone makes heirlooms valuable.

Lucy Larcom, *A New England Girlhood*, 1889.

In the last ten years there has been a new interest in quilts in America. As works of folk tradition and folk art, quilts are enjoying a steadily growing respectability. The craft itself is undergoing something of a revival, and the numerous books published, and museum exhibitions sponsored, during the past five or six years on various aspects of the quilt and quilting attest to the increased attention Americans are paying to this antique craft.

At least part of the reason for this new appreciation lies in the rediscovery of the true quality of design and workmanship represented by this art form. As anyone who has seen some of the late nineteenth-century Amish quilts will confirm, both the design and the craftsmanship incorporated in quilting can be spectacular. But the immediacy of a quilt's function—as an object intended to provide warmth, comfort, protection and visual satisfaction in the home—cannot be separated from its artistic merit. A quilt's original function as a household object increases its value for twentieth-century Americans; quilts are particularly rich and suggestive artistic statements because of their individual and collective associations.

The children's and dolls' quilts in this collection—objects made for or by children —evoke rich connotations; for the experience of being a child is a particularly fascinating subject for contemporary American adults. Ours is a culture very conscious of its children, of the formative stages of development; to a large extent it is youth-centered. Childhood is a universal experience, but it is also a personal and individual one: it both includes us in part of a culture and distinguishes us as individuals. Psychology has made us aware of the importance of our individual experiences as children in the development of our adult personalities; it is natural that the objects of childhood, the games, toys, clothing, or articles made by adults for the comfort or nurture of children, should hold special charm for us and appeal to us in strong ways.

The idea that America is a youth-centered society is not new. British travelers to this country in the late nineteenth century found the license given children by American parents fairly appalling, while others thought this freedom signalled a beneficial, though revolutionary, social trend. At least one Englishman thought youthful impertinence and precocity revealed disregard for age, wisdom and tradition, and implied that the unparalled attention Americans paid their young would destroy the established order and stability of a properly hierarchical society. Others saw the arrogance and liberty of American children as the living application of the new American theories of equality: the democratic character of the society was to be insured by providing its children with freedom and mobility.

America's focus on its young, and through them on the future, has important implications. Looking toward the future may make possible new modes of behavior and activity, but it may create a lack of stability and cultural permanence. It may be that this lack causes us to depend more heavily on personal memories for a sense of connection with the past. Possibly this is why, as a culture, we are intrigued by the objects and symbols of childhood, both our own and those of others. One way of clarifying values in an everchanging present is to reclaim values of an established, unchangeable past.

The American historian John Demos has said that "much can be learned of a culture by investigating the way it regards its young." Moving away from an exclusive interest in public events toward a more comprehensive study of private and individual experience, historians are coming to focus more attention on the common man and woman—and child—and less on the upper class members of any historical period. As one of these historians, Tamara Hareven, has expressed it, "The renewed interest in the field [of family history] . . . undoubtedly also received its impetus from a series of recent crises relating to the conflict between generations, the rebellion of youth, the changing status of women, and growing doubts and anxieties over the future of the family."

To explore the common person's experience, historians are looking more closely at such documentary sources as diaries, letters, business accounts and records, the vital records of towns (where births, deaths and marriages of a community were recorded), land deeds and titles, and church records. These sources, when used together, add pieces to the historical puzzle, and illuminate the individual lives of average people in an historical time period.

At the same time, the general American public is coming to value more highly the physical artifacts of past lives: furniture, household tools and farm implements, toys and clothing, and hand-made items of all description are currently in great popular

demand, and the new popular interest in quilts is part of this trend. These products of the past help us understand the experiences of individuals in a cultural context, and twentieth-century Americans are looking for ways to place their own personal experience in some social, political or historical context. The renewed enthusiasm for such handcrafts as quilt-making are reflections of the larger impulse to understand the experience of everyday life in the past.

We would like to place these quilts made for children in the context of nineteenth-century life. By looking at various artifacts and documents relating to the experience of children, we may understand the functions these quilts might have filled in their time: How were they used? What did they mean to the children for whom they were made? Who made quilts for infants, and what did making a quilt for a child signify to the mother or grandmother or older sister who pieced it?

CHILDHOOD
IN THE NINETEENTH CENTURY

. . . *Begin early* is the great maxim for everything in education. A child of six years old can be made useful; and should be taught to consider every day lost in which some little thing has not been done to assist others.

Children can very early be taught to take all the care of their own clothes.

They can knit garters, suspenders, and stockings; they can make patchwork and braid straw; they can make mats for the table, and mats for the floor; they can weed the garden, and pick cranberries from the meadow, to be carried to market.

Lydia Maria Child, *The American Frugal Housewife*, 1832.

If childhood is a particularly compelling area for study, it is also a particularly elusive one. How can we bring childhood experiences to life? Children do not speak to us of their own perceptions in conventional, adult terms. Rather than reflecting on and generalizing about their personal histories, they react and respond to their surroundings in a more immediate way, often using fantasy and role playing to try out new ideas or new patterns of behavior. While we may look at childhood as a period of experimentation and creativity, children's games and models are frequently imitations of adult culture. In our efforts to understand a child's experience, particularly in the past, we find relatively few means of directly reconstructing a child's world.

It is not surprising that children kept relatively few diaries, and that few of those accounts survive. There are, however, some direct accounts of a child's daily experience in late eighteenth- and early nineteenth-century America. A rather expansive diary was kept by Elizabeth Fuller, the daughter of a minister who lived in Princeton, Massachusetts. Elizabeth, the third daughter in a family of five girls and five boys, writes the following in April, 1791.

> 1 I wove two yard and three quarters and three inches to-day and I think I did pretty well considering it was April Fool Day. Mr. Brooks and Mr. Hastings here to get Pa to do some writing for them.

4 I wove five yards and a quarter. Mr. Cutting here this eve.

5 I wove four yards. Mrs. Garfield and Mrs. Eveleth who was once Caty Mirick here a visiting. The real estate of Mr. Josiah Mirick deceased is vendued to-day.

(eve) Timmy has got home from the vendue. Mr. Cutting has bought the Farm gave 225 £ Sam Mathews has bought the part of the Pew gave eight dollars.

6 I got out the White piece Mrs. Garfield warped the blue, came here and began to draw in the Piece.

7 I finished drawing in the Piece and wove a yard and a half. Sam Matthews here to-day.

15 I began to spin Linnen spun 21 knots. I went to Mr. Perry's on an errand. Pa went to Mr. Matthews to write his will and some deeds. He has sold Dr. Wilson 20 acres of Land and given Sam a deed of some I believe about 25 acres.

Throughout the diary, Elizabeth records her spinning and weaving, evidence of her economic contribution to the family's income, as well as the level of her skills. Elizabeth's interest in and knowledge of her father's business reminds us that the father's work was very much in evidence in the early nineteenth-century farming village, in contrast to today. Elizabeth's awareness of these transactions reflects her sense of herself as both a family member and a member of a larger community.

Detailed though it is, Elizabeth Fuller's diary is a record of individual events, rather than a generalized and reflective account of her experience. While it is vivid and suggestive in its own right, we need more. Keeping this diary in mind, we can begin to piece together a more complete picture of childhood in America in the early-nineteenth century.

In the early part of the nineteenth century, the vast majority of American families lived on farms or agricultural communities. This meant that most families sought to provide for their needs from the produce of their land, their livestock and their household activity. They traded what surplus goods they produced on the farm for desired manufactured goods, and imported articles, at the local village stores. In this way, each family functioned as an economic unit, and each member had a role to play.

Before 1840, most children took on significant responsibilities as workers in the family economy at about the age of six. Before that time, a child was considered an infant, and spent most of his or her time learning the rhythms of the family. Even though children as young as three might be sent to district school in the winter months, they spent most of their time at play. The playground for these children was the family farmhouse and farmyard. Until the age of five or six they probably stayed within the range of their mother's work area, playing in the kitchen or a nearby bedroom, or in the area just outside the kitchen where chickens or a cat might be sources of amusement. Child life during this time was not without its hazards, as the number of deaths by scalding or fireplace burns recorded in towns' vital records testifies, but it was not without its pleasures.

Children took their part in adult tasks. Families during the early nineteenth century had an average of five to nine children, usually spread at about two-year intervals, and while approximately one fifth of these infants died within the first two years of birth, the majority of children who survived their first ten years lived to maturity and even old age. So a middle-aged couple might have as many as four or five youngsters between the ages of four and sixteen all working on the farm at different tasks according to their age and sex. In addition, the family might have an infant in its crib and a child away from home, apprenticed to a craftsman, or attending college, or working in a textile mill. The children living at home assisted their parents in all the activities of the farm: in processing crops during the winter, in hoeing fields and tending the garden during the growing season, in feeding the animals or helping in their slaughter, in working flax and wool, and learning to spin and weave. The activity of the family was the work of the family, and children began to learn their tasks at an early age.

The nuclear family provided for the education, social development and religious training of the young child. The prime function of the family was economic, and the role of both the mother and the father was to provide their children with basic hand and technical skills. In addition, parents were responsible for the formation of the children's moral characters. The child, in turn, contributed to the economic well-being of the family from an early age. In this sense, the young child was expected to take on the role of a small adult, and thus we can say that the society at this time was comparatively adult-centered.

The second half of the nineteenth century witnessed vast changes in all aspects of the American society into which Elizabeth Fuller had been born. Industrial development (particularly textile manufacture), the dramatic growth in native and immigrant populations, the growth of towns and cities, rapid advances in transportation and communications, and the settlement of Western lands combined to radically transform life for the average American family.

The technological revolution and the growth of mill communities and large urban centers, particularly in the New England and mid-Atlantic states, brought about important changes in the agricultural communities. Concentrations of people in commercial centers created new markets for farmers, and the increased manufactured goods available in stores stimulated trade. This, coupled with the settlement of Western land which created farm produce—especially good wheat—to compete with the crops of the East, caused farmers in the coastal states to specialize in their produce.

Dairying, sheep-raising, and truck farming became specialties; the farmer found that in order to compete he either had to concentrate all his energies on the output of his fields, or acquire a trade related to farming. For a farmer to combine farming with a craft became less common, and the early nineteenth-century's integrated work patterns became obsolete.

Just as important a change in daily activity occurred in rural women's lives. Industrialization brought about a decline in women's economic function. With the wide availability of inexpensive, commercially manufactured textiles, the woman's role as family textile-producer diminished. In addition, her production of surplus butter, cheese, vegetables and textile goods—which had been used as important exchange items in the family's store account—became insignificant contributions to the farm income. Women's domestic activities were no longer income-producing; the elimination of home textile production symbolized the shift in women's economic role from producers to consumers. Simultaneous with this shift was a shift in men's roles from workers within the family to workers outside and away from the family. As the nineteenth century progressed, the mother of the family became the exclusive keeper of the household and the father became the exclusive provider of the income.

Not only was farming and farm life changing, but fewer people were living on farms. By the middle of the nineteenth century, Americans were moving into cities in increasing numbers. City life created different roles for family members; city children did not often participate in the economic functioning of the middle class family. When children did work, it was usually at very different tasks from those their parents performed, and likely at some distance from them. Industrialization meant more geographic, social and economic mobility for individual Americans; it meant increased opportunities for work and more variety in occupational choices. It also meant that the fathers' work became distinct from the housework of mothers and children, and adults' activity became removed and isolated from that of their children. The continuity between generations was broken, and this break led to a change in the way Americans dealt with their children. In order to cope with a changing, increasingly complex world as modern adults, children needed to be treated (and trained) differently than they had been when children looked forward to a life very much like that of their parents.

Children lost their importance as economic producers for the family in this new technologically specialized society, and stopped learning economic and professional skills from their parents' activities. Therefore new institutions for incorporating children into the adult society and for training them in technical skills needed to be created. A child of seven or eight could no longer accompany his father into the fields and learn his work at first hand; adult male work became more specialized and excluded those who did not have the manual or mental dexterity of adults. Children now needed places where they could learn the technical skills they would need as adults.

This situation was slightly different for young girls, but only slightly. Girls still learned some housekeeping skill directly from their mothers, but the weight of responsibility for the raising and training of yet another generation of modern children would all-too-quickly fall to these "little women," and it was felt by parents that the more general education girls received, the better prepared they would be to function as the wives and mothers of future generations.

So children were sent to schools to learn, not only the reading, writing and cyphering they had once learned at district schools, but also technical skills. The new institutions created for this kind of training were outside the family and required that children leave the home. High schools were developed in the mid-nineteenth century to accommodate this need for further formal education not available at home; trade schools and academies proliferated for young men, and normal schools and finishing schools became common for girls.

Sarah Jane Bradley attended and boarded at the Abbott's Institution at 49 Bleecker Street in New York City in 1849. She was probably about thirteen when she wrote the following entry in her journal:

> Alice and I took out our worsted embroidery this fore-noon, and I have
> done little else today, but work worsted and pick my work out again.
> Encouraging.

Sarah Jane is definitely learning specialized, refined skills which will identify her as an accomplished young woman. But she will use these skills more to fill the leisure hours that her increasingly modernized world will provide her than to bring economic or social benefit to her family. On another day, Sarah Jane comments:

Drawing from Nature, both with pen and with India ink, is the all absorbing subject of Mr. Jacob's department, at present. One hears nothing but "designs," designs from morning till night. Tumblers, goblets, lamps and such like things are all-in requisition. Mr. Jacob has established an "Arts-Union" on the plan of the "American Art Union."

Here a girl is learning esthetic appreciation and, potentially, skills of interior design and ornamentation. Sarah Jane, unlike Elizabeth Fuller, is not learning to spin linen and wool; she anticipates, and her parents anticipate for her, a sheltered life in which artistic sensibilities will be valued.

By the late nineteenth century, change was one of the few constants for middle class Americans. Basic technological innovations transformed the early-nineteenth-century world and brought a new kind of diversity and instability to the lives of individual Americans. The economic productivity of the family lost its direct relationship to the rhythms of the seasons and the hand skills of its adult members. It gained an intensified dependence on nationwide (and even worldwide) market fluctuations and business activity.

It is almost impossible to sketch the typical experience of a child growing up in the late nineteenth century, because the society was no longer unified by the everyday patterns of preindustrial society. Individual experiences began to diverge sharply; people were affected by a wide set of variables. Where one lived, what one's father did for a living, how much access one's family had to both private and public modern conveniences: these factors began to figure centrally in the shaping of a child's experience, and differentiated one child's youth from another's.

The late nineteenth-century family was not an institution through which a child was gradually and gracefully introduced into the adult society. It was an institution which served to physically nurture and protect its children, and bolster them emotionally for the discontinuities they would face "outside." During a period of rapid change and increasing specialization, parents could not be sure that their skills would be applicable to the adult lives of their children. As formal education and vocational training took over the traditional functions of apprenticeship and informal education at home, parents focused on helping their children develop personal habits, the character which would help them adapt to changing situations. Eventual entry into the world of adulthood was assumed, but the age of entry was postponed significantly, and the dependent and youthful stages were prolonged. Adults became more concerned about the child's passage into maturity, and more attention was paid this slow passage.

CHILDREN'S COMFORT, ADULT'S COMFORT

Another trial confronted me in the shape of an ideal but impossible patchwork quilt. We learned to sew patchwork at school, while we were learning the alphabet; and almost every girl, large or small, had a bed-quilt of her own begun, with an eye to future house furnishing. I was not over fond of sewing, but I thought it best to begin mine early.

So I collected a few squares of calico, and undertook to put them together in my usual independent way, without asking direction. I liked assorting those little figured bits of cotton cloth, for they were scraps of gowns I had seen worn, and they reminded me of the persons who wore them. One fragment, in particular, was like a picture to me. It was a delicate pink and brown sea-moss pattern, on a white ground, a piece of a dress belonging to my married sister, who was to me bride and angel in one. . . . I could dream over my patchwork, but I could not bring it into conventional shape. My sisters, whose fingers had been educated, called my sewing "gobblings." I grew disgusted with myself, and gave away all my pieces except the pretty sea-moss pattern, which I was not willing to see patched up with common calico. It was evident that I should never conquer fate with my needle.

Lucy Larcom, A New England
Girlhood, 1889.

In recent years, many people have voiced concern over the decline of the family in modern America; such trends as the rising divorce rate and declining birth rate are often cited to suggest that the family has lost its importance. Historians of the family, however, suggest that the functions of the family, and therefore the meaning of the family, has simply shifted. As America modernized, the child's economic importance diminished; the family became primarily concerned with the child's emotional and psychological development. Providing for the child's comfort became increasingly important. The greater number of quilts in this exhibition are from the later nineteenth century, and reflect that society's concern for the comfort of its children.

The primary purpose of these quilts was to provide warmth for a child in a cradle or crib. Quilts may also have been placed on the floor as padding for infants who were too young to crawl, as is common in our own day. A number of the older quilts seem to be worn on the pieced side rather than on the backing, which

4. CHILD'S QUILT
c. 1885
found in Alfred, Maine
44″ × 39″
Made up of nine printed cotton kerchiefs of English and American origin of red, white and black.
Collection of Professor Matthew Wysocki

would support this conclusion. The elaborate designs and juxtaposition of colors undoubtedly served to amuse and stimulate the small child learning to distinguish patterns and color, and we can speculate that these quilts became symbols of comfort for their users as they moved into later stages of childhood.

As the child grew older, quilts took on a different significance. Many older children mastered the process of quilt-making themselves, and some of them created quilts for younger siblings. In *The American Girl's Book*, printed in 1831, we find this suggestion:

> Little girls often find amusement in making patchwork quilts for the beds of their dolls, and some even go so far as to make cradle-quilts for their infant brothers and sisters.

(This passage is followed by directions for a hexagon patchwork quilt strikingly similar to the one on page 2.) It seems likely that this kind of participation in the preparations for a new baby comforted the older child and gave him or her a sense of responsibility for and connection to the infant.

A quilt can provide comfort for the small child who uses it; the making of a quilt can give its creator a sense of satisfaction. For women in the late nineteenth century, this was especially true. By making a quilt, a mother could express in a concrete way her concern for the physical and emotional well-being of a child. In addition, she could demonstrate her skills both to her family and to other members of her community. The availability of commercial quilt-making kits and packages of silk and satin remnants in the late nineteenth century suggests that quilt-making during this period was not so much an act of economic necessity or thrift as it was an exercise in esthetics. Finally, the piecing of a child's quilt by a mother, female relative or friend established the maker's personal connection with the traditional hand processes and people of the past. The author of *The Ladies' Hand Book of Fancy and Ornamental Work*, Florence Hartley, presented this viewpoint by saying:

> We own to a liking for Patchwork, genuine old-fashioned patchwork such as our grandmothers made, and such as dear old maiden aunt, with imperfect sight, is making for fairs and charities, and whiling away otherwise tedious hours.

In an age when the Sears and Roebuck Company was selling inexpensive bed coverings of all description, including machine-made quilts, the making of a child's quilt became largely an act of sentiment, a way of expressing one's affection for a child, a means of feeling connection with the traditions of the past. Symbols of the security of the home, each of these quilts speaks to us of both an adult's and a child's comfort.

Notes

Introduction

[1] Lucy Larcom, *A New England Girlhood* (Gloucester, Massachusetts, 1973), p. 149.

[2] Richard Rapson, "The American Child As Seen by British Travelers, 1845–1935," *The American Family in Social-Historical Perspective*, ed. Michael Gordon (New York, New York, 1973), pp. 192–208.

[3] "Developmental Perspectives on the History of Childhood," *The Family in History*, ed. Theodore K. Rabb and Robert Rotberg (New York, New York, 1973), p. 127.

[4] "The History of the Family as an Interdisciplinary Field," *The Family in History*, ed. Theodore K. Rabb and Robert Rotberg (New York, New York, 1973), p. 212.

Childhood in the Nineteenth Century

[1] Lydia Maria Child, *The American Frugal Housewife* (Boston, 1832), p. 4.

[2] Francis Edward Blake, *History of the Town of Princeton, Massachusetts, 1759–1915* (Princeton, Massachusetts, 1915), p. 308.

[3] We are indebted to Nancy Osterud's unpublished paper, "The New England Family, 1790–1840" for many of the ideas expressed in this chapter, as well as to countless conversations with both former and current staff members at Old Sturbridge Village.

[4] See John Demos and Virginia Demos, "Adolescence in Historical Perspective," *The American Family in Social-Historical Perspective*, ed. Michael Gordon (New York, 1973), pp. 209–221 for more information on this topic.

[5] Journal of Sarah Jane Bradley. Typescript at New York Historical Society, p. 31.

[6] Ibid., p. 19.

Children's Comfort, Adults' Comfort

[1] *A New England Girlhood*, p. 122-124.
[2] See Aries, pp. 9–10.
[3] Jane Nylander, Curator of Textiles at Old Sturbridge Village, suggested this idea to us initially.
[4] Eliza Leslie, *The American Girl's Book* (Boston, 1831), p. 299.
[5] Florence Hartley, *The Ladies' Hand Book of Fancy and Ornamental Work* (Philadelphia, 1859), p. 189.

Bibliography

Primary Source materials

Beecher, Catharine E. *Treatise on Domestic Economy for Use of Young Ladies at Home and at School.* Boston: Thomas H. Webb and Co., 1842.
Beecher, Catharine E., and Stowe, Harriet Beecher. *American Woman's Home*, or *Principles of Domestic Science.* Hartford: Stowe-Day Foundation, 1975. (First published in 1869. New York: J. B. Ford and Co.)

69.—The Quilting Bee.

Courtesy of America Hurrah Antiques

Blake, Francis Edward. *History of the Town of Princeton, Massachusetts, 1759–1915*. Princeton: 1915. (Excerpts of Elizabeth Fuller's diary available through Old Sturbridge Village.)

Child, Lydia Maria. *The American Frugal Housewife*. Boston: Carter, Hendee and Co., 1832.

Diary of Sarah Jane Bradley, 1849. Typescript at New York Historical Society, New York, New York.

Hartley, Florence. *The Ladies' Hand Book of Fancy and Ornamental Work*. Philadelphia: 1859.

Larcom, Lucy. *A New England Girlhood*. Gloucester, Massachusetts: Peter Smith, 1973. (First published in 1889.)

Leslie, Eliza. *The American Girl's Book*. Boston, 1831.

The Housekeeper's Weekly.

Secondary Source Materials

Aries, Philippe. *Centuries of Childhood*. Translated by Robert Burdick. New York: Random House, 1962.

Beels, C. Christian. "Whatever Happened to Father?" *New York Times Magazine*, August 25, 1974.

Bremner, Robert H., ed. *Children and Youth in America: A Documentary History*. Vols. I and II. Cambridge: Harvard University Press, 1971.

Demos, John. *A Little Commonwealth: Family Life in Plymouth Colony*. London: Oxford University Press, 1970.

Gordon, Michael, ed. *The American Family in Social–Historical Perspective*. New York: St. Martin's Press, 1973.

Orlofsky, Patsy and Myron. *Quilts in America*. New York: McGraw-Hill Book Co., 1974.

Osterud, Nancy. "The New England Family, 1790–1840." An unpublished paper. (Available through Old Sturbridge Village.)

Rabb, Theodore K., and Rothberg, Robert I., eds. *The Family in History: Interdisciplinary Essays*. New York: Harper and Row, 1973.

Color Plates

5. HEART AND HAT
    c. 1850 Yonkers, New York
    34½″ × 32½″
    Appliquéd with chintz borders. Above hat is written "Phoenix
    Factory"; under it, the word "Yonkers." Above and below the
    heart is written (with minor variations in the wording): "A Heart
    I send you Squire Baldwine/Reject it not I do implore thee/A
    warm reception may it meet/My name a secret I must keep";
    signed, "Old Maid."
    Collection of David L. Davies

6. APPLIQUED OAK LEAF WITH TULIP
    AND FLOWERS
    c. 1860
    Pennsylvania
    38″ × 38″
    Red and green oak leaves with tulips and flowers are appliquéd
    on orange cotton background, with zigzag and cable quilted
    border.
    Collection of Phyllis Haders

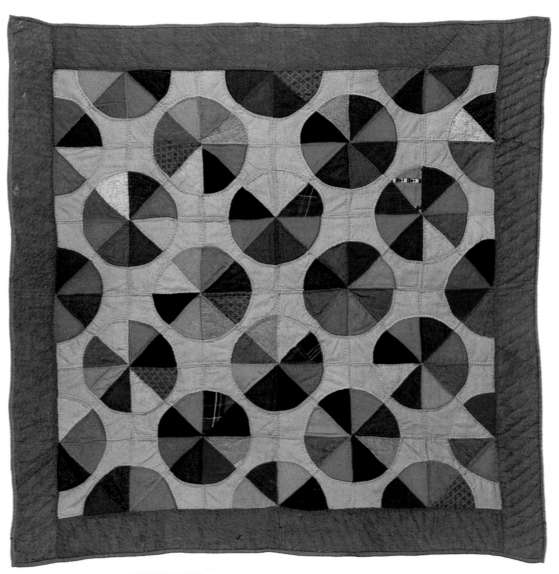

7. PINWHEEL
c. 1890
Amish
Pennsylvania
36½″ × 37″
Multicolored fabrics form repeated pinwheel design throughout.
Collection of America Hurrah Antiques

8. BASKETS WITH HANDLES
c. 1880
Pennsylvania
43″ × 48″
Basket pieced with appliquéd handles; pink, blue and green cotton with three-sided pink and blue sawtooth border.
Collection of Gloria List Antiques

9. FRIENDSHIP ALBUM QUILT
c. 1876
42″ × 35″
Maker: Mary B. Hayes
Pink and white cotton with triangular sawtooth border.
Calligraphic needlework with poem dated 1876.
Collection of America Hurrah Antiques

10. LOG CABIN, LIGHT AND DARK
c. 1899
Pennsylvania
37½″ × 38″
Rectangular strips of light cotton fabric interspersed with dark
fabric form four distinct diamond shapes.
Collection of Thos. K. Woodard: American Antiques and Quilts

11. LOG CABIN, COURTHOUSE STEPS
c. 1875
New England
40½" × 41"
Multicolored cottons compose this dark and light log cabin design.
Collection of Thos. K. Woodard: American Antiques and Quilts

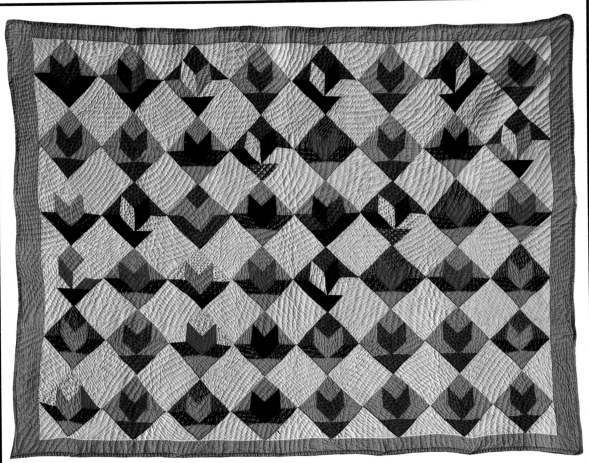

12. COURTHOUSE STEPS
c. 1875
Mennonite
York County, Pennsylvania
47½" × 42"
Multicolored solids and cotton calicoes form Courthouse Steps which consist of 1700 ½" strips set on a blue background.
Collection of Jonathan Holstein and Gail van der Hoof

13. CACTUS BASKET
c. 1880
Pennsylvania
43" × 56½"
Multicolored pieced cotton cactus design with orange border.
Collection of Gloria List Antiques

14.   LONE STAR
c. 1890
34″ × 35″
Tiny green and red stars against white cotton background with
detailed quilting and red and white sawtooth border.
Collection of Mr. and Mrs. Frank J. Miele

15. CHINTZ CUTOUT
1863
Michigan
30″ × 29″
Heart-shaped chintz cutouts are appliquéd on white cotton background with floral border signed in quilting, "M.C.R. Susanna,
1863."
Collection of America Hurrah Antiques

16. SUNFLOWER
c. 1840
Connecticut
37″ × 38″
Pink, brown and white pieced cotton forms diamond and triangular shapes of center motif.
Collection of Phyllis Haders

17. DIAMOND IN THE SQUARE
c. 1880
37″ × 33″
Pieced cotton. Pink, red and black diamond-formed squares set
on white background alternating with brown floral squares.
Collection of Chase Manhattan Bank

18. ROMAN STRIPES
c. 1910
Ohio
34″ × 41″
Multicolored pieced silk stripes form twelve diagonal blocks set into silk vertical and horizontal bars surrounded by a black border.
Collection of Bryce and Donna Hamilton

19. FEATHERED PLUME
1880
Pennsylvania
46″ × 48″
Trundle quilt. Feathered oak leaf with birds appliquéd on bright
orange background. A Prince's Feather variation, of cotton.
Collection of Phyllis Haders

20. PYRAMIDS, DOLL QUILT
c. 1890
Maine
11″ × 14″
Indigo blue pyramids alternating with red and white stripes with
patterned pink and white border. Cotton.
Collection of Gloria List Antiques

21. STARBURST
c. 1900–10
Pennsylvania
41″ × 41″
Vivid multicolored cotton triangular shapes form this starburst pattern.
Collection of Phyllis Haders

22. POTS OF PUFFED FLOWERS
c. 1820–30
Newark, New Jersey
39½″ × 40½″
White cotton, top ornamented with four pots of puffed flowers.
The appliquéd flowers are of pink, yellow and red sprigged cotton.
Fan-patterned quilting throughout. The quilt descended in the
Morris family of Washington Street, Newark.
Collection of the Newark Museum

23. PRINCESS FEATHER
c. 1860–70
44" × 45"
Appliquéd in red, yellow and green on blue cotton background
with red, yellow and blue repeated in border.
Collection of Richard and Rosemarie Machmer

24. BASKETS AND EIGHT-POINTED STAR
c. 1870
New York City
29½″ × 38½″
Red and white cotton triangular pieced baskets with blue-green
eight-pointed appliquéd stars on white background.
Collection of Gloria List Antiques

25. STAR OF BETHLEHEM
1930 Arthur, Illinois 50″ × 37½″
Amish
Cotton fabric made by Bertha Schrock. Yellow, pink and green
diamonds form this star pattern set on a blue cotton background,
with diagonal borders.
Collection of Jonathan Holstein and Gail van der Hoof

26. CRAZY QUILT
c. 1880–90
39½″ × 39″
Cotton and wool with large rooster embroidered in center motif.
Collection of George E. Schoellkopf Gallery

27. TUMBLING BLOCKS WITH
CRAZY QUILT BORDER
c. 1889–90
Vermont
52″ × 54″
Multicolored silks and patterns form the center tumbling blocks, with a border in a crazy quilt pattern and fan shapes in each corner.
Collection of Thos. K. Woodard: American Antiques and Quilts

28. KANSAS BABY
c. 1861
Nebraska
36″ × 36¾″
Homespun, hand dyed, pieced and appliquéd in red, white and
blue with "BABY" embroidered in center star.
Collection of Phyllis Haders

29. PIECED AND APPLIQUED QUILT
c. 1875
44″ × 35″
Pieced and appliquéd house forms center motif flanked on left and
right with leaf and floral ribbon trees on which birds are set. Three
stars are appliquéd on white sky background with sun coming over
the mountain. Cotton.
Collection of Miss Christophe de Menil

30. **STARBURST**
    c. 1830
    46″ × 48″ (framed)
    Pieced cotton and appliquéd cutout chintz birds in four corners
    with Ohio Star border. Star of Bethlehem variation.
    Collection of George E. Schoellkopf Gallery

31. **CHECKERBOARD, DOLL QUILT**
    c. 1910–20
    Iowa
    19″ × 19″
    Red, white and blue checkerboard diamond effect in cottons with
    red, white and blue striped border.
    Collection of Gloria List Antiques

32. EIGHT-POINTED BROKEN STAR
Ulster County, N. Y.
29″ × 29″
Flying geese border with red, white and green cotton calico.
Collection of Mrs. Davis O. Harrington

33. LOG CABIN VARIATION, DOLL QUILT
c. 1865–70
Pennsylvania
12″ × 22½″
Multicolored cotton prints are used to form this pattern.
Collection of America Hurrah Antiques

34. APPLIQUED CHILD'S QUILT
c. 1920–30
Kentucky
46″ × 61″
Pieced multicolored windmill, numbers, alphabet, and house on white quilted background with floral appliquéd border.
Collection of Robert Shallow

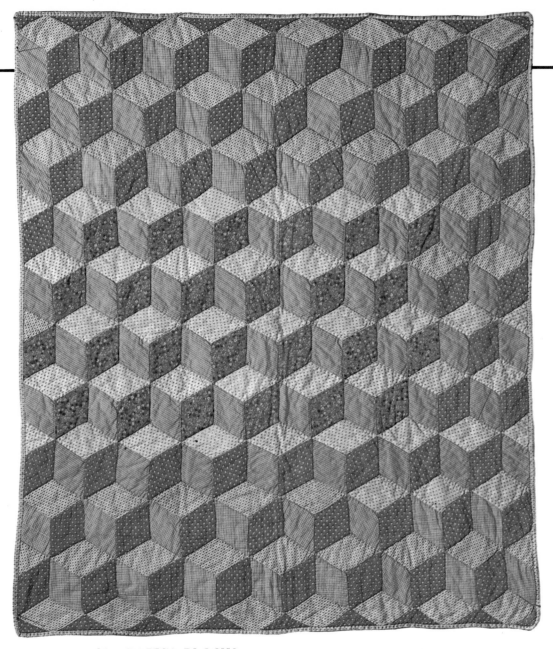

35. BABY'S BLOCKS
c. 1860
New York
29″ × 34″
Tricolored fabrics form all-over diamond-shaped pattern design.
Collection of Phyllis Haders

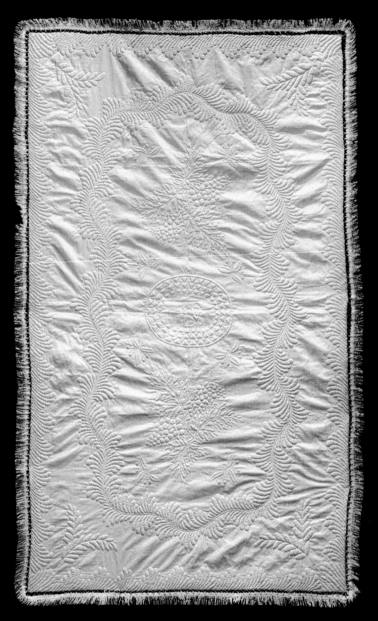

36. WHITEWORK
c. 1850–60
Newark, New Jersey
60" × 35½"
Maker: Meta Colt Toler. Her initials are cross-stitched in red and
on the upper right corner of the back. White cotton top. At the
quilt's center within a floral medallion is a realistic horse outlined
in backstitch. Arranged around the horse are embroidered berries
and quilted grape clusters. Quilted feather vines form the border.
All details of the design are stuffed with cotton, no filling in other
areas; white linen backing; edge bound with white cotton fringe.
Finest example of machine-made sewing.
Collection of the Newark Museum

37. WHITEWORK
c. 1825
New England
33″ × 28″ (6″ fringe)
White muslin quilted and stuffed with center motif of basket with
fruit and grapes. The quilt is finished on three sides with a 6″
fringe border.
Collection of America Hurrah Antiques

38. SUNBURST
c. 1850
33½″ × 34″
Chintz cutouts form center motif with pieced sawtooth and appliquéd border.
Collection of Thos. K. Woodard: American Antiques and Quilts

39. NINE PATCH
c. 1880 Amish Ohio
31″ × 41″
Black and purple cotton fabrics form this nine patch block set on
black background. Purple and black borders reverse to magenta
backing.
Collection of Barbara S. Janos and Barbara Ross

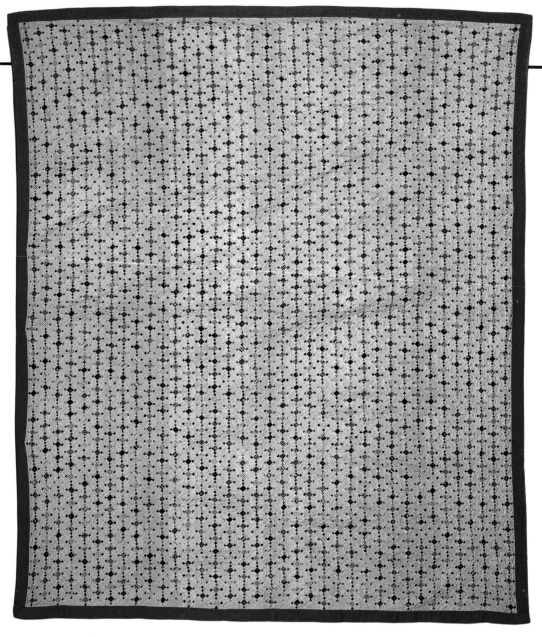

40. MINIATURE NINE PATCH QUILT TOP
c. 1880
Maplewood, New Jersey
74″ × 64″
Maker: Emma Atkinson, the daughter of John D. and Frances J.
Atkinson of Maplewood. The quilt was made for Emma's brother
Charles. Extraordinary piecing workmanship. Typical nine patch
design set between printed cotton triangles in 37 bands of multi-
colored cottons. Red cotton border.
Collection of the Newark Museum

41. MOSAIC CRIB QUILT
c. 1880
Pennsylvania
Amish
30″ × 40″
Composed of hexigons in multicolored silks arranged in many
groups with sawtooth border.
Collection of Marcia and Ron Spark

42. DELECTABLE MOUNTAINS
c. 1880
New Jersey
38" × 56"
Red and green cotton pieced work on white background with
double red and green sawtooth border.
Collection of Gloria List Antiques

43. CHINESE COINS
     c. 1904–10
     Amish
     Ohio
     32″ × 57″
     Multicolored cotton and wool horizontal bars alternate with solid
     maroon stripes. Black sateen border finishes off this unusual child's
     quilt.
     Collection of Barbara S. Janos and Barbara Ross

44. LOG CABIN DAZZLER
c. 1880–90
New Jersey
42″ × 42″
Log cabin in center motif with alternating bars, stripes and saw-tooth border in multicolored silks.
Collection of Molly Epstein

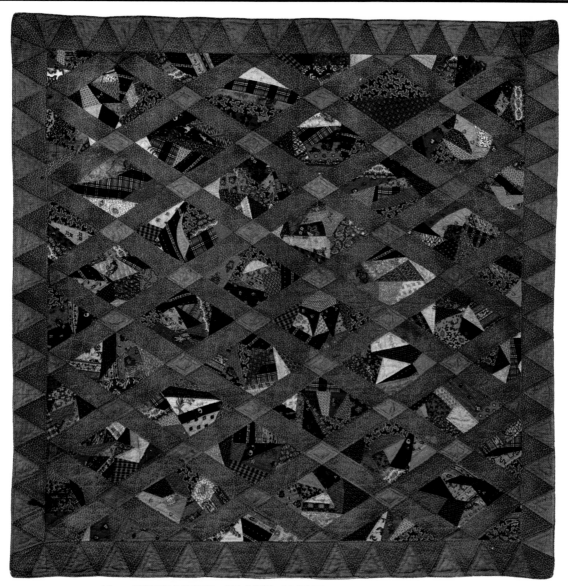

45.   CONTAINED CRAZY QUILT
c. 1835
Pennsylvania
44½″ × 45″
Cotton chintz and various multicolored roller-printed cottons make
up this unusual crazy quilt pattern.
Collection of America Hurrah Antiques

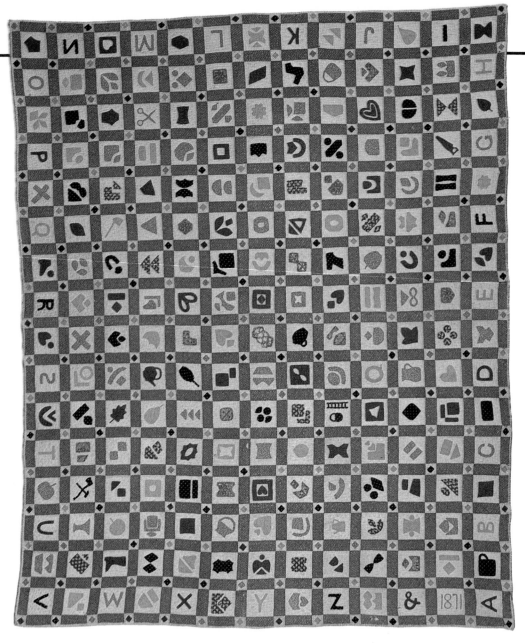

46. CHILD'S QUILT, APPLIQUED AND PIECED
1871
New York State
62″ × 77″
Virtually a child's primer composed of 208 cotton blocks with
each block consisting of realistic and abstract designs.
Collection of Thos. K. Woodard: American Antiques and Quilts

47. FOUR PATCH
c. 1900
Amish
Pennsylvania
Lancaster County
41″ × 39″
Purple and brown woolens form diamonds which are set onto
green background with red and black borders.
Collection of Jonathan Holstein and Gail van der Hoof

48. ALBUM CHILD'S QUILT
c. 1850–55
New York
42" × 52"
Each block consists of realistic objects appliquéd on white cotton background, including a man holding an American flag.
Collection of America Hurrah Antiques

49. DOLL BED AND DOLL QUILT
Bed: c. 1850
Long Island
wood
Quilt: c. 1850
Long Island
18½" × 25"
American one patch forms four pink flowers interspersed with white, green and blue patches with blue triangular border. Cotton.
Collection of Joanna S. Rose

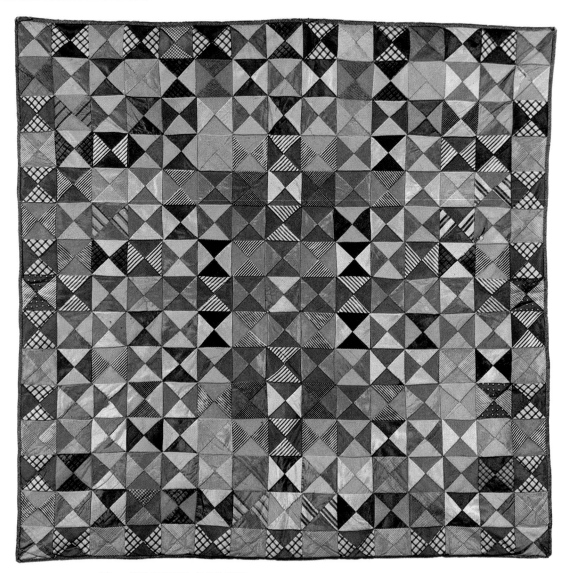

50. BROKEN DISHES
c. 1850
30¾″ × 32″
Four triangular shapes form each square of this multicolored silk
all-over pattern.
Collection of Phyllis Haders

51. CRAZY QUILT
c. 1880 Bennington, Vermont
42″ × 61″
Multicolored silk, velvet and brocade heavily embroidered with
animals and flowers. Hexagonal maroon velvet center motif with
handpainted rose.
Collection of Tony Ellis and Bill Gallick

52. BISCUIT PATTERN CRIB QUILT
c. 1820
Bedford, New York
49″ × 50½″
Maker: Miss P. Reynolds
Stuffed raised work form frames for the pictorial appliquéd designs in this quilt: Lily of the Valley, Compass, Wanderer's Path in the Wilderness (Drunkard's Path), Tree of Paradise, Cactus Blossom, Bird of Paradise, Royal Japanese Vase, Blazing Star, Star of Bethlehem, Old Folks at Home to Dinner, Old Log Cabin, Spruce, Two Stumps, Rose of Sharon, Pineapple, Dog Days, Stars, Sun and the Covenant, June Lip, Evening Star.
Collection of the Bedford Historical Society

PART II:

How to Make Your Own Child's Comfort

by Josephine Rogers

Before You Begin

Many people who are interested in making a child's quilt do not know quite how to begin. This portion of the book serves two purposes:

1. to provide an understandable beginner's guide on pattern designs, colors, and fabric selection;
2. to offer the seasoned sewer, quilt maker, and needlewoman three traditional designs represented in this book.

Many of the quilts represented in this book are composed of pieces in:

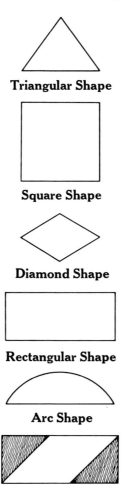

Triangular Shape

Square Shape

Diamond Shape

Rectangular Shape

Arc Shape

Parallelogram Shape

Some are made using appliqué; others utilize a technique called whitework, a quilting design drawn on white muslin, quilted in white thread and stuffed at various intervals (trapunto).

Before you begin your own child's quilt, ask yourself these practical questions: who is the quilt for and what size quilt am I making?

Measurements for Another Person's Quilt

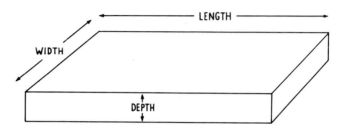

If you are making a quilt for another person's child or baby, or to give as a gift, here are some standard measurements to use as a guide:

Standard Sizes

Infant	20″ x 36″ or 36″ x 54″
Bunker or cot	33″ x 74″
Child	48″ x 68″
Single bed	39″ x 74″

Measurements for Your Own Child's Quilt

If you are making this quilt for a member of your own family, begin by measuring the length and width of the mattress for which the quilt is intended, from corner to corner along each side. Now measure the depth (that is, how thick the mattress is) and double this measurement, since the quilt will cover both sides. Now decide how much of an overlay you want—that is, how much do you want the quilt to hang beyond the mattress? If you want the quilt to hang to the floor, measure from the end of the mattress to the floor, double this dimension and add this measurement to the length, width, and depth measurement you already have. If you want the quilt to tuck under the mattress, add 3″ to 4″, double this dimension and add to your other measurements. For more length at the top of the quilt to allow for pillow underlay, allow 7″ and add to lengthwise measurement only.

Fabrics and Their Selection

Many types of fabric are used in the quilts represented in this book. Woolens are used in the crazy quilt on page 43, while silks and satins form the center log cabin motif with diagonal and sawtooth borders in the quilt on page 61. However, the majority of quilts represented in this book are made of 100-percent cotton.

Cotton remains the finest and most durable type of natural fabric to be used for your child's quilt. Cotton fabrics are smooth-textured, finely woven, easily maintained, and have a greater tensile strength (stretching quality of yarn as fabric is being woven) than any other fabric. If you are unable to find 100-percent cotton fabric easily, you may choose fabrics which are 50 percent cotton and 50 percent Dacron, to use in combination with other cotton fabrics. If you do, remember to preshrink all of your fabrics, as even today's cottons can shrink 1 to 2½ percent.

If you are uncertain of your fabric's content, it is wise to wash it in a hot water cycle before using, to avoid possible future shrinkage.

Cotton fabric comes in many different patterns and weights. The best type of cotton to use in your quilt should be medium weight, such as broadcloth, calico, chambray, chintz (as seen in the quilt made of chintz cutouts on page 32), gingham, percale, poplin, sateen, sheeting (which may be used in part for quilt tops and for backing), and velveteen (which may be combined with satins and silks and should not be laundered, as this type of fabric can ravel quite easily).

You may be as adventuresome as you like in selecting your fabric pattern, but do consider these basic design elements:

1. the pattern design you have selected for your quilt;
2. the color and scale of the patterns used in the fabric;
3. the number of pieces used.

After you have gathered this information, it may be helpful to you to know that the most popular printed or woven patterns are gingham checks, floral prints, dots, stripes and calico prints. What you select will depend on your individual taste. But if you are still uncertain about the use of colors and fabrics in your child's quilt,

53. CRIB QUILT
c. 1870
Plymouth, Massachusetts
29″ × 35″
Composed of cotton, multicolored stripes and triangles and diamond shapes.
Collection of Esther and Christopher Pullman

look at the photograph on page 59 and see the interesting ways in which fabric colors and patterns have been intermingled. You may need to know where to get fabric for your quilts. But remember, since this craft grew out of necessity, it is wise to use first all the fabrics you have on hand (fabrics from old garments may be used if not worn too thin). Then ask your friends and relatives, and everyone you know, if they have any scrap fabric. Finally, and only as a last resort, go out and buy fabric, and if you do, buy a little extra. There is nothing more frustrating than having to stop in the midst of your cutting to run out to buy extra fabric.

Color

Color influences all our lives. We all wear the colors we like, and surround ourselves with the most satisfying colors in our homes. Color has a great psychological influence on our lives, too. Some colors help us feel joyful, others sad.

Whether you are making this quilt to remain in your own family, or to be given as a gift, with care it should last a lifetime; and this means that every aspect of your total quilt look should be considered. In order to have the most pleasurable color experience while working on your quilt, consider these questions:

1. Is your quilt being made for a boy or a girl? Bed coverings need not be limited to the pastel pinks and blues formerly associated with little girls and boys. If you would like to use a group of brilliant colors do so. If you wish to use an unconventional color story, as seen in the purple and black Amish quilt on page 56, that's all right too. If you do use pink or blue, make certain it is used in combination with other colors, as in Baby's Blocks, on page 52. As you can see, there is a contrast between light and dark tonal qualities. Each color complements its neighboring color and produces an all-over effect that is visually exciting.

2. Is the quilt to be the focal point (center of attention) of the room? Then use plenty of bright reds, yellows, blues and greens with touches of orange; for a more subdued effect, use quieter colors such as pale yellows, blues, pinks and greens.

3. Is there any sunshine in the child's room, or will the room be darkened most of the day? As a rule, northern rooms are cooler, because they lack direct sunlight, and northeastern rooms have sunlight only during the morning hours. In this case, you may choose to use reds, yellows and oranges with touches of grass green and robin's-egg blue. On the other hand, if your child's room is brightened by streams of sunlight through

54. DOLL QUILT AND DOLL BED
Quilt: c. 1850–60
Pennsylvania
12½″ × 13″
Appliquéd star and leaves on white cotton background.
Bed: c. 1860
Pennsylvania
Polychromed wood
Doll: c. 1850
Pennsylvania
Stuffed cotton rag doll.
Collection of Jonathan Holstein and Gail van der Hoof

southern or southwestern exposure, you may wish to select cooler colors—turquoise blue, sea green or lemon yellow. Here touches of red and orange can be added for contrast; if this is too bright, it can be toned down by using navy blue, chocolate brown, and even splashes of black as a contrast (if used sparingly).

Whatever colors you decide to use, think brightly and remember that the colors you've selected may be the child's first visual experience and influence his or her life far more than you may imagine.

Tools of the Trade

Before you begin your quilt you will need:

1. Scissors that are sharpened to cut a clean line.
2. Pins, $1\frac{1}{4}''$ (larger than standard pin size is necessary when pinning together two thicknesses of fabric and stuffing).
3. Needles: long needles for basting; short ones for quilting.
4. Thread: for basting and quilting.
5. Thimble: one that fits easily on your middle finger, a must for quilting; otherwise you will get a little hole in that finger.
6. Brown paper: for your paper pattern cut to the size of your finished quilt.

For measuring:

1. Transparent plastic ruler, 12″ long and 1″ to 2″ wide.
2. Wooden or metal yardstick.

For making templates:

1. Cardboard.
2. White bond paper (for paper patterns).
3. Graph paper.
4. Rubber cement.
5. Sharpened pencils.

55. CHINESE COINS WITH HEARTS AND FLOWERS
1976
New York City
32″ × 57″
Maker: Josephine Rogers
Tiny hearts and flowers are intermingled with brightly colored
solids and other printed cotton fabrics to form horizontal bars alternating with navy blue vertical stripes quilted in cable stitch. Red
and navy blue borders are quilted with tear drop pattern. Navy
blue end borders are quilted with hearts and flowers.
Collection of Josephine Rogers

CHINESE COINS

The quilts that you see in this book were made by different people and represent a wide cross section of pattern designs, fabrics and colors. Possibly these quilters copied patterns that already existed, such as the Star of Bethlehem, Log Cabin and Baby's Blocks. Others created completely original designs of their own, such as Lady of the Lakes and Feathered Oak Leaf.

As far as your child's quilt is concerned, careful consideration should be given to the selection of your pattern design. This design should be based on your own sewing skills, rather than on what you would simply love to make. For example, in the Double Pyramid design quilt, notice the finely detailed piecing and appliqué, and the delicacy of the quilting. Sewing a pattern design of this type requires a certain kind of finger dexterity that will take time to develop. On the other hand, a simple pattern like Chinese Coins requires only simple sewing skills.

This quilt belonged to the family of an Amish bishop. It was their best quilt and was placed on their child's bed only on Sundays after church services, when their home was opened to parishioners.

The origin of the name Chinese Coins is a little bit puzzling. A friend has said that the pattern has been in her family as long as she can remember. She had heard that a relative had created this free-form design to resemble the Chinese devices used to count out change, hence the name Chinese Coins.

At first glance the bishop's Chinese Coins quilt may appear rather dark and somber. However, remember that the Amish used these dark colors as part of their traditional religious background, which dates back to the fifteenth century. This simple pattern design can be made more visually exciting by the use of such bright colors as red, yellow, green, blue, purple, orange and pink, adding touches of calico and tiny floral prints. The use of these colors and fabrics in alternating vertical strips and horizontal bars can give your child's quilt a greater sense of brightness and design than the Amish version.

You can make your own modern-day version of Chinese Coins, as I did.

I call my quilt "Chinese Coins With Hearts and Flowers." I used a small floral print with hearts and flowers, intermingled with bright solid-color fabrics and other prints.

To Begin

Refer to the section on fabric selection as to the type of fabric to use. Cut a paper pattern the size of your finished quilt, 32″ wide by 52″ long. Cut five vertical strips in navy fabric 39½″ long by 3″ wide. Cut about 144 to 174 3″-wide pieces of fabric, in random lengths, from various solid-color and print fabrics, to form the six 39½″-long rows of horizontal bars. There should be about 24 to 29 of these horizontal bars in each row. Measurements include a ¼″ seam allowance.

Lay the strips and bars on the paper pattern as shown in the illustration below:

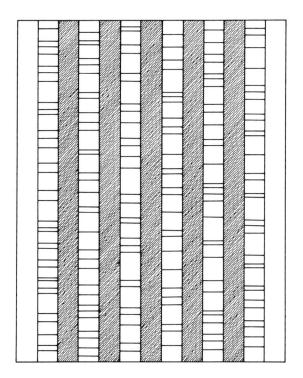

Move the colors around until you have achieved an effect pleasing to your eye. Now pin all the strips and bars in place to the paper pattern. This paper pattern represents a road map to follow in pinning, sewing and joining your quilt top. When you are not working on your quilt, the paper pattern with the fabric pieces pinned to it can be rolled up and put away, and everything will be in place when you unroll it to work on your quilt again.

Sewing and Joining

Using your paper pattern as a guide to show the sequence in which your quilt top is to be assembled, pick up your horizontal bars, starting with the top of the center row. Pin the first bar to the second, with right sides together; continue in this manner until you have a long strip of bars. Sew them together with a $\frac{1}{4}''$ seam allowance in either a small running stitch or machine stitch set at 8. Press all seams flat with a downward motion. Let's call this central row Row #1.

Now pick up the solid vertical strip to the left of Row #1. This is Row #2. Pin and sew it to Row #1, with a $\frac{1}{4}''$ seam allowance. Rows #1 and 2 are now joined. Next, pick up the vertical strip to the right of Row #1. This is Row #3. Pin and sew it to Row #1 on the right side.

Continue in this manner until all of the bars and strips have been joined, pinning, sewing and pressing as you go. When you have joined the last row, the center section of the quilt top will be complete.

Now you are ready to begin cutting the light and dark rectangular pieces to form the inner alternating borders (see illustration on page 43). Cut 6 light and 4 dark rectangular pieces $2\frac{3}{4}''$ wide and $6''$ long (adding $\frac{1}{4}''$ seam allowance along all outer edges). Cut 4 dark pieces at $4\frac{1}{2}''$ long (adding $\frac{1}{4}''$ seam allowance). Pin 3 light and 4 dark pieces together alternately end to end to form a pinned strip. Use $4\frac{1}{2}''$ dark pieces on the ends of the strip. Sew together horizontally with $\frac{1}{4}''$ seam allowance. Press seams flat with a downward motion. Pin the strip to the left side of the center section of your quilt top with $\frac{1}{4}''$ seam allowance. Sew the strip to the center section vertically. Press flat toward center of quilt top. Repeat these steps to form right side of alternating borders, pinning, sewing and pressing flat toward center section.

Now you are ready to cut the solid-colored outer borders. Cut 2 strips of fabric $2\frac{1}{2}''$ wide by $39\frac{1}{2}''$ long (adding $\frac{1}{4}''$ seam allowance along all outer edges). Join these vertical strips to the center section of your quilt top (with $\frac{1}{4}''$ seam allowance) by pinning, sewing and pressing flat toward the center.

To form horizontal end borders, cut 2 pieces of solid-colored fabric $30\frac{1}{2}''$ wide by $6\frac{1}{2}''$ long, adding $\frac{1}{4}''$ seam allowance along all outer edges. Join these end pieces to center section of quilt top horizontally by pinning, sewing and pressing flat toward the center.

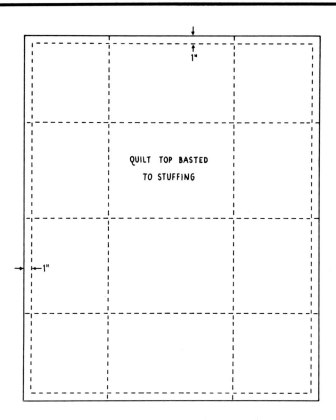

Joining Quilt Top to Stuffing

Lay the straightened quilt top on the stuffing, making certain that all outer edges are perfectly straight. Pin top and stuffing together, working outward from the center, pinning and smoothing at intervals as you go. Baste quilt top to stuffing vertically and horizontally, down the center, and along each outer edge 1″ in from the edge.

Joining Backing to Quilt Top and Stuffing

Cut backing fabric 36″ wide by 54″ long (1″ larger on all sides than quilt top— the extra fabric will be folded over to form a border). Place quilt top face down on table and join backing to it, pinning, smoothing and basting in exactly the same

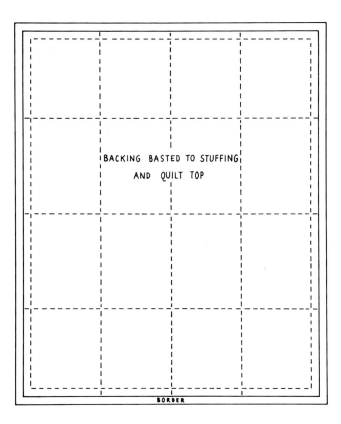

BACKING BASTED TO STUFFING
AND QUILT TOP

BORDER

manner as with stuffing. Turn quilt face up so that the patchwork is again on top. Turn under a $\frac{1}{2}''$ hem from back to front all around backing. Fold backing from back to front onto patchwork top to form a $\frac{1}{2}''$ border. Pin in place, leaving four corners free from mitering. Miter corners by turning fabric under at a 45-degree angle. Pin, baste and stitch in place, using double-duty thread.

Finishing Your Quilt

Now that your quilt is completed, you will have to tuft it together to keep it from coming apart during washing. The illustration (on the next page) shows how this is done.

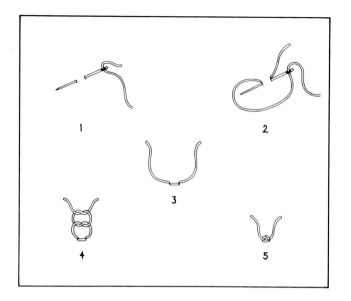

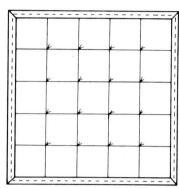

How to Tuft

To tuft, thread a large-eyed needle with Knit-Cro-Sheen thread. Starting at quilt back, pass the needle through the three layers (just catching seam at various intervals), leaving a $2\frac{1}{2}''$ tail of thread on backing side for tying. Bring needle up again, close to the first point. Repeat stitch in same place for extra strength, ending on backing side of quilt. Tie threads in a square knot. After all threads are tied, clip to even $1\frac{1}{2}''$ lengths. Remove all basting stitches from quilt.

Quilting Guide

For those people who are experienced hand sewers, or quilters, below you will find a pattern that I used to quilt Chinese Coins. Notice that I used soft, flowing patterns of Cable Stitch and Teardrop to break up the sharp vertical and horizontal lines of the piecing. For the borders I used small hearts intermingled with flowing flowers.

In order to mark in your quilting pattern, cut a paper pattern measuring 40″ long by $1\frac{3}{4}''$ wide, and draw a Cable Stitch pattern on it similar to that shown in the illustration. Pin this pattern on the vertical strips of the quilt and, with a sharp-pointed pencil, perforate holes along the lines of the pattern. Mark these points on the quilt with light-colored pencil (on dark fabric) or No. 3 pencil (on light-colored fabric). Quilt with short running stitches.

For light and dark vertical borders, draw in Teardrops as indicated in illustration and quilt with same color thread as background fabric.

For wide end borders, cut a heart-shaped template 1¾" long by 1⅝" wide. Place on quilt and trace around it as indicated in illustration. Then draw in three flowers on each end border in flowing free-form pattern, as illustrated. Quilt with short running stitches.

Bind off with a bias strip cut from same color fabric as border. Stitch into place.

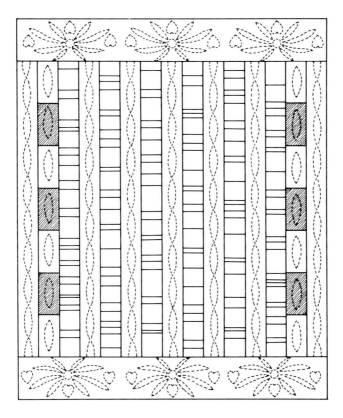

Now that you have finished your quilt, be sure to identify your work by embroidering on it your name, the date, and the place where the quilt was made. This insures that someone picking up your quilt 100 years from now will not have to say "Hmmm—I wonder who made this quilt?"

56. WINDMILL BLADES, LOG CABIN
c. 1870
Pennsylvania
34″ × 43″
Light and dark cotton and cotton sateens with red center square
motif.
Collection of Gloria List Antiques

LOG CABIN

Another design pattern I find exciting is the Log Cabin. This design uses contrasting rectangular strips of light and dark color tones.

The pattern of each block is built around a center square with narrower rectangular pieces surrounding the center. These blocks can be placed in many different ways, but notice the interesting arrangement in the Log Cabin design shown here:

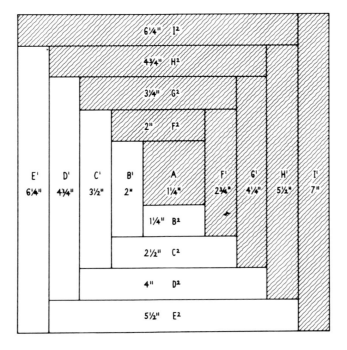

In order to make this Log Cabin design, you will need to make templates for each individual piece. It may seem like a lot of trouble to begin with, but you will save time in the end if you cut templates for all of your pieces. This means that you will have to make 17 templates in all (but since they are reusable, with care they could last a lifetime).

Take graph paper and mark out one square and 16 rectangular strips, according to the dimensions shown in the Cutting Guide on the next page.

Cutting Guide for Templates

Template A (square) 1¼″ x 1¼″

B-1	2″ x ¾″	**F-1**	2¾″ x ¾″
B-2	1¼″ x ¾″	**F-2**	2″ x ¾″
C-1	3½″ x ¾″	**G-1**	4¼″ x ¾″
C-2	2½″ x ¾″	**G-2**	3¼″ x ¾″
D-1	4¾″ x ¾″	**H-1**	5½″ x ¾″
D-2	4″ x ¾″	**H-2**	4¾″ x ¾″
E-1	6¼″ x ¾″	**I-1**	7″ x ¾″
E-2	5½″ x ¾″	**I-2**	6¼″ x ¾″

Identify each template with the corresponding letter and number and an L (for light) or D (for dark) according to the fabric to be cut with it (see Cutting and Sewing Guide). After you have measured and marked all 17 templates, glue the graph paper to a piece of cardboard with rubber cement. When dry, cut out templates evenly along the lines, using paper scissors, making certain to be precise in your cutting. Remember, if your pieces are cut crooked, your blocks will be crooked and your quilt will look crooked.

Cutting and Sewing Guide for Log Cabin Quilt

A—Dark red, navy, brown, maroon (used as accent colors)
B, C, D, E—Lighter colors such as beige, gray, cream, bright red
F, G, H, I—Darker colors such as purple, brown, rust, maroon

Since the Log Cabin quilt is usually made of scrap fabric, trace and cut out 16 pieces of various types of fabric from each template. You will have a total of 272 pieces—16 center squares, 128 strips of light-colored fabrics, and 128 strips of dark. You will note that in the Log Cabin quilt in the photo on page 27, the pairs of strips corresponding to B-1/B-2, C-1/C-2, etc., are cut from the same fabric. This creates the strong geometric diamond pattern in this quilt. If you wish to achieve the same effect in your quilt, use identical fabric for strips 1 and 2 in each letter grouping. Otherwise, use any scrap fabrics of the same tonal value to produce the light and dark effects.

When cutting your pieces, remember to add ¼″ seam allowance along outer edges in each dimension. Check your Cutting and Sewing Guide to determine which pieces to cut in each color group. Sort your pieces into 16 groups of 17 pieces each, one for each block of the quilt.

Take brown paper and cut a paper pattern 36½" by 36½" square. This represents the size of your finished quilt. Cut 16 blocks of preshrunk muslin 7½" by 7½" square. Take a group of 16 pieces and sew them to a muslin block as follows: Start piecing in the center by sewing strip B-2 to square A, using a ¼" seam allowance then joining strip B-1 to square A, and continuing to sew around in a counterclockwise direction, using your Cutting and Sewing Guide as a check. When all the strips have been sewn to the muslin block, the finished block should measure 7½" by 7½" square. Continue until all 16 blocks have been sewn.

Take one block and place it in the lower right-hand corner of your paper pattern. This is Block #1. Now take another block and place it to the left of Block #1. (See Joining Guide for proper alignment of blocks.) This is Block #2.

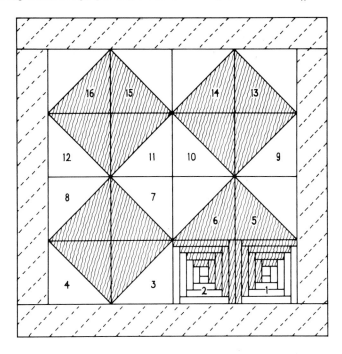

Joining Guide

Using the Joining Guide as a check, lay all the blocks on your paper pattern and pin them in place. The pattern can be rolled up when not in use, keeping your work flat, neat and easily referable.

When all blocks have been laid out, pick up Block #1 and Block #2 and sew them together, using a ¼″ seam allowance and pressing the seam flat (see Joining Guide for direction of pressing). Then join Block #3 to Block #2, and Block #4 to Block #3. Continue in this manner until you have four rows of blocks.

Now join Row #1 to Row #2, using ¼″ seam allowance, and press the seam flat in one direction. Join Row #2 to Row #3 and Row #3 to Row #4. Now that all of your blocks are joined, add a 5″ border along all outer edges of your sewn blocks. Straighten quilt top with a yardstick. Your quilt top is now completed.

For backing, cut one piece of fabric 39″ by 39″. Turn in edges of backing ½″ all around and press. With wrong sides together, pin backing to quilt top, matching folded edge of backing to quilt top. Slip-stitch pieces together. Tuft from back to front through both layers at all corners where four blocks meet, tying knots on backing side. (See "How to Tuft," p. 84.) Press all outer edges lightly.

57. CRAZY QUILT, DOLL SIZE
c. 1880
31″ × 31½″
Multicolored silks, velvets and damask with flowers embroidered in the four corners and with a 1½″ velvet border.
Collection of Susan Grant Lewin and Harold Lewin

BABY'S BLOCKS

This lovely tricolored design (see p. 51) is made up of three diamond shapes which compose each individual block. Different optical effects can be achieved by changing the color placement. Notice how in this Baby's Blocks pattern the eye is moved in a zigzag direction by the use of red calico, pink-and-white striped, and white-dotted fabrics. However, if a solid blue fabric were used instead, along with a yellow print and blue-and-white-dotted fabric, a completely different optical effect would be achieved.

To make your tricolor fabric selection more visually exciting, be sure to use strong contrasts of light and dark fabrics.

Cut out a paper pattern 34″ wide by 29″ long (the size of your finished quilt). Now you are ready to begin your Baby's Blocks quilt.

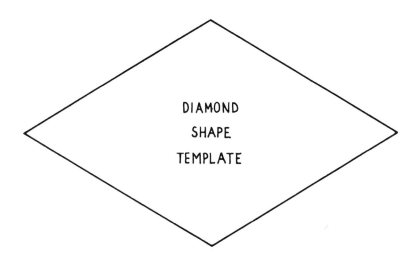

DIAMOND
SHAPE
TEMPLATE

Cut out the pattern above and use it as a guide for making a template. Make certain that ¼″ seam allowance is added each time you trace around the template on fabric (as this pencil line is your ¼″ seam allowance and sewing line). Now check the Cutting Guide to see the exact number of diamond shapes to cut for your Baby's Blocks quilt.

Cutting Guide

Cut the following pieces:

83 whole diamonds of white-dotted fabric
80 whole diamonds of pink-and-white striped fabric
80 whole diamonds of red calico fabric
10 half diamonds (cut crosswise) of white-dotted fabric
14 half diamonds (cut lengthwise) of red calico fabric
 4 small triangles (half of a half diamond) of red calico fabric

Check the photograph on page 52 for exact angles and placement of pieces.

Using ¼″ seam allowance, join Diamond Shape #1 to Diamond Shape #2. (See Joining and Pressing Guide below.) Press seams flat. Now join Diamond Shape #3 to Diamond Shapes #1 and 2. This forms one complete Baby's Block (Block A).

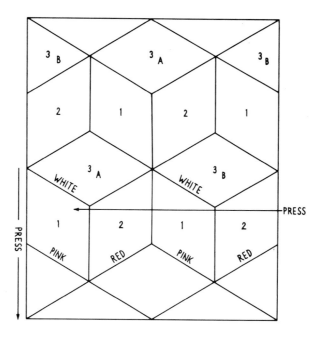

Joining and Pressing Guide

Continue in this manner, joining three diamond shapes of different colors to form each individual block. When the second block (Block B) has been completed, join it to Block A. Continue in this manner until one row of blocks has been completed. Lay this row of blocks at the top of your paper pattern. This is Row #1.

Continue joining, sewing and pressing blocks together to form Row #2. When it has been completed, join Row #2 to Row #1, as shown in the diagram below.

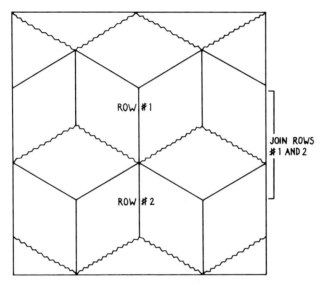

Continue in this manner until ten rows have been completed and joined together.

Now fill in the edge rows of the quilt with the half diamonds and triangles, fitting the four small red calico triangles into the corners. Refer to photograph on page 52 for exact placement of pieces. Your quilt top is now completed. Straighten all outer edges carefully.

Lay quilt top on stuffing and cut stuffing same size as your finished quilt top. Baste in manner described on page 82.

Mark in quilting pattern in light-colored or white pencil. Quilt in pattern as shown in the diagram on the next page.

When quilting has been completed, you are ready to bind off. Cut a bias strip $3\frac{1}{2}$ yards long by $1\frac{1}{2}''$ wide from contrasting fabric (white fabric was used in this quilt). Pin along raw edge of quilt, allowing $\frac{1}{4}''$ seam allowance. Stitch into place.

STAR OF BETHLEHEM

Many Early American quilt patterns took their inspiration from Bible stories and religious imagery. The Star of Bethlehem, also called Star of the East, is a bold geometric pattern whose name recalls the brilliant star that led the wise men to the infant Jesus. This pattern has also been called "Lone Star," to celebrate the solidarity of Texas with the Union.

Traditionally this pattern is made with diamonds of solid-color fabric in light and dark color tones alternating with calico prints. Notice that in this pattern design all the diamond shapes are made of solid-color fabrics of pale yellow, rose pink and pale green.

This is not by any means a simple pattern. But if you wish to duplicate this Star of Bethlehem, you will need ½ yard each of pale yellow, rose pink and pale green cotton fabric (50% cotton and 50% Dacron may be used) to form your diamond shapes. For border and binding, you will need 2 yards of bright blue fabric 45″ wide. For backing, you will need 1½ yards of 45″-wide fabric. If you wish, four alternate colors of your own selection may be used. If this is the case, make very certain that there is a strong contrast between the dark and light diamond shapes and the background color.

Cut a paper pattern 39½″ wide by 54″ long. This represents the size of the finished quilt. As you complete the various component parts of this quilt, place them on your paper pattern, and you will see this quilt literally grow before your eyes.

Trace paper diamond pattern to form central Star of Bethlehem. When you cut out your fabric diamonds using this pattern, make certain to add ¼″ seam allowance along each outer edge.

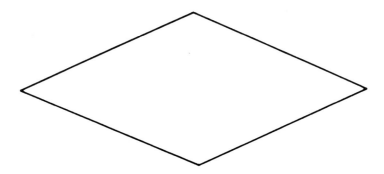

Cutting Guide for Center Star

Cut the following pieces:

40 diamonds of pale yellow
64 diamonds of rose pink
24 diamonds of pale green

Cutting Guide for Diagonal Square Border

Cut the following pieces:

18 diamonds of pale yellow
19 diamonds of rose pink
19 diamonds of pale green

Fit triangles into corners wherever necessary.

Cutting Guide for Diagonal Border Bars

Cut the following pieces:

10 diamonds of pale yellow
10 diamonds of rose pink
10 diamonds of pale green

Add triangular shapes when necessary to fill out ends of borders.
NOTE: Separate all pieces according to color.

After you have cut all of your diamond shapes, you are ready to begin piecing (sewing) your diamonds together, with a $\frac{1}{4}''$ seam allowance. Pick up pieces according to Color Guide on the next page.

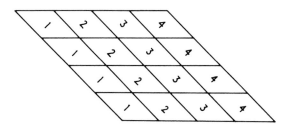

Color Guide

A. pale yellow
B. rose pink
C. pale green

Consult Piecing Guide for the order in which to sew the diamond shapes together. This piecing will form the first section of the eight-pointed Star of Bethlehem.

Piecing Guide

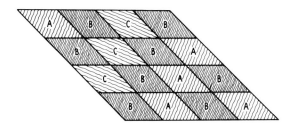

Usng ¼" seam allowance, sew diamonds together horizontally. Press seams flat in a downward motion. Continue in this manner until 4 rows of diamonds have been joined. Now join Row #1 and Row #2 diagonally and press flat towards the center. Continue in this manner until all diagonal seams have been joined. When first section of star has been completed, lay on paper pattern. Continue until eight separate sections of the eight-pointed star are completed. Now join the eight sections together, as shown in the diagram on the next page.

Your Star of Bethlehem is completed. Lay it on the paper pattern to keep neat and wrinkle-free while you work on the other parts of your quilt.

To form square and triangular insets, cut four square shapes 8½" by 8½", and four triangular shapes 11½" by 8" by 8" from bright blue fabric, adding ¼" seam allowance along each outer edge. Set square and triangular inset pieces into eight points of Star of Bethlehem and sew in place, using ¼" seam allowance. Press seams flat in downward motion.

Sew diamonds together to form square border. Press flat in one direction. Sew border to center star section.

Cut four pieces of bright blue fabric 5½" wide by 39" long, adding ¼" seam allowance. Join to center star section, alternating the solid pieces with the diagonal border bars.

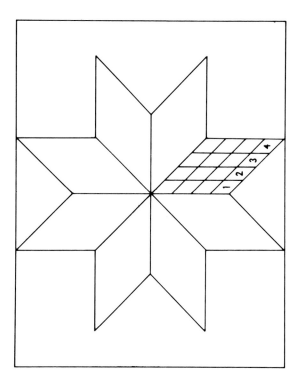

Now cut two pieces of bright blue fabric 5½″ wide by 54″ long and join vertically along outer edges of quilt with ¼″ seam allowance. Press flat towards the center. This completes the border for your quilt top. Straighten outer edges carefully.

Lay quilt top on stuffing and cut stuffing same size as your finished quilt top. Baste in manner described on page 82.

For backing, cut out one piece of fabric measuring 39½″ wide by 54″ long and baste to quilt top and stuffing in above manner.

Mark in quilting pattern in light-colored or white pencil. Quilt in pattern as described in Quilting Guide on the next page.

When quilting has been completed, you are ready to bind off. Cut bias strip 5½ yards long by 1½″ wide (these measurements include ¼″ seam allowance). Pin along raw edge of quilt, allowing ¼″ seam allowance. Stitch into place.

Quilting Guide

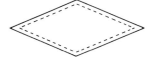

1. Quilt ¼″ in from outer edge of each diamond.
2. Quilt flower design in corners and between points of star.
3. Quilt tulips between border and bars.
4. Quilt in cable stitch border.

From the boys and girls
of the
Light Brigade
of
Grace Lutheran Church
Beth., Pa. Oct. 1924

CARING FOR AND DISPLAYING QUILTS

Baby and doll quilts are easy to make if you follow a pattern. The four traditional patterns in this book—Chinese Coins, Log Cabin, Baby's Blocks, and Star of Bethlehem—show what elements a pattern should include if you wish to design one yourself, perhaps working in motifs that have, or will have, special meaning for your own family. Here a few quilt motifs to consider:

Stuffed Animal Toys. Teddy bears, pandas, bunnies, kittens, and other fuzzy animal toys can be quilted into a spread. Use the animal as a central sculptural element and create a patchwork background around it. The stuffed animal can be new or one of the child's long-time favorites that is long past its proper time of retirement because of overuse. Many children will find a quilt that incorporated an old toy very reassuring at night.

The Word "Baby." The word "baby" was often worked into quilts by pregnant women because they did not know the name or sex of the child they were carrying. The simpleness of the word highlighted the exquisiteness of the lettering used in many examples. Such quilts usually formed part of a layette.

Alphabets, Names, and Monograms. To individualize any quilt, the child's name or the doll's name can be quilted onto the fabric. This is most effective when used as a repeat border. The name is embroidered over the quilting, or perhaps over some of the outside seams. If you want to use one or two letters or even a short name, such as TOM or SUE, you should consider stuffing that section of the fabric. This technique is called trapunto, and while not often used in traditional quilts, it is quite acceptable for adapted quilts or modern quilts that are modifications of traditional designs. The idea is to stitch around the design that is to be stuffed, then carefully insert small amounts of torn, wadded, or shredded stuffing into the secured area. This is most easily done with a crochet hook or knitting needle and often requires great patience. The filled and sculpted shape is then closed with a few stitches and tacked to the backing of the quilt.

58.   ANIMAL QUILT
      1924
      Beth, Pennsylvania
      56″ × 48″
      dated October 2, 1924
      36 blocks with animals embroidered in red thread on white cotton backgrounds are set together to form this quilt top. Signed: "From the boys and girls of the Light Brigade of Grace Lutheran Church, Beth, Pennsylvania, October 2, 1924."
      Collection of Mr. and Mrs. Morris Firtell

59. UNDERGROUND RAILROAD, DOLL QUILT
c. 1850
New York State
19″ × 22½″
Red triangles and squares form an all-over pattern on white cotton
background with red binding. Tufted in white silk thread
Collection of Joanna S. Rose

60. CARPENTER'S SQUARE, DOLL QUILT
c. 1850
Pennsylvania
Red strips form square motif with intersecting right angles. Heavily
quilted throughout with wide cable stitched border. Cotton.
Collection of Joanna S. Rose

Baby Events. Cross-stitched alphabets in block letters and script letters can also be used to individualize a quilt. A small quilt-sampler could be most effective to record the name, date, and birth weight of an infant. It would provide the basic statistics to any interested admirer who want to know about the baby.

Quilted Doll and Baby Clothes. Pieces of baby clothes or fabrics that were used in swaddling have traditionally been used in the construction of baby coverlets. This is a variation of that idea: quilt an exquisite but outgrown hat, bootee, or even an entire christening dress into a baby quilt. The garment should make up the center of the modern quilt and might also have other baby motifs in evidence. This requires the same techniques as suggested for the animal quilts.

Care of an Antique Quilt. Antique quilts vary as much in condition as they do in pattern. No two, even with the same pattern, are alike. Some have been carefully stored in lined trunks or packed away in durable boxes, safe and secure in dry attics or undisturbed in dry cellars; others have fared less happily.

If you have found your antique quilt in a flea-market or bazaar, or perhaps spotted it in a bundle of rags (a treasured find), your quilt is probably in bad repair and needs a major overhauling with reseaming and restuffing. The first job, then, is to carefully assess the condition of the quilt and decide what the problems are, and note the solutions that are possible. Good mending and repair can bring many quilts that are little more than shreds back to service and a semblance of their former beauty. And, perhaps the worn quilts are all the more charming for the wear. However, there is nothing charming about grease stains, especially on a baby or doll quilt.

The first step is to shake the quilt or patchwork pieces thoroughly but gently to loosen any caked-on dirt. If possible, air the quilt in open air and sunlight for at least six hours. Sunlight will allow you a chance to note and measure the problems and at the same time get rid of musty odors, and even some possibly unwanted guests who have made their home in the quilt.

Most common of all stains on quilts and bedding are "foldmarks." If the fabric has been folded, a yellowish stain will mark the crease and extend into the surrounding area delineating the fold. These marks can usually be dissipated by washing and will fade as the entire quilt is exposed to air.

Mold is the next most common stain problem. Mold is associated with mildew which is a parasitic fungus growth. It appears when there is moisture, stale air, and a continuous dank, damp environment or excessive humidity. It appears as dull brown splotches which disfigure the fabric and weaken the fiber. The ugly patches resemble a strange skin disease with a scattering of dark brown spots varying in size and density with shading usually lighter at the edges. Since mold is a fungus that must eat to live,

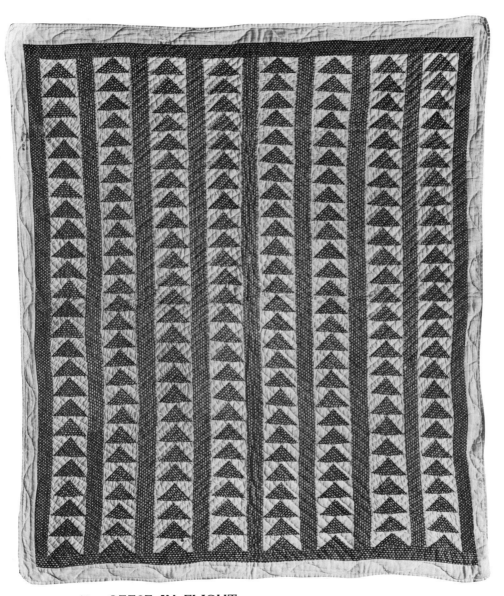

61. GEESE IN FLIGHT
c. 1880–90
New York State
32″ × 36″
Blue and white pieced cotton form the Geese in Flight pattern.
Each section is separated by alternating vertical blue bars with a
blue and white border.
Collection of Thos. K. Woodard: American Antiques and Quilts

mold is most often found on fabrics that have been starched or that have been sized —especially with cornstarch.

The first step is to dry the quilt or fabric as carefully as possible by exposing it to circulating air and sunlight. If sunlight is not possible, place the quilt across a rack or chairback in the path of an electric fan or some other air-moving device.

Air pollution, the same villain that clogs lungs and causes respiratory problems can seriously affect quilts. Some quilts in perfect condition for almost a century seem to age rapidly—in a few years—when exposed to air pollution. The quilts used as wall hangings in urban areas are the most exposed.

Sulphur dioxide, the gas given off by burning fossil fuels such as gasoline and oil, is the chief cause of pollution. There is probably no way to escape the perils of pollution but the effects can be minimized. Framing the quilt, keeping it covered, and storing it in a sealed plastic bag or an air-tight container helps.

Insects can cause damage to delicate fabrics. Dank fabrics are perfect homes for cockroaches, silverfish, termites, worms, and undesirables. Here again the best defenses are sunlight, dry atmosphere, and securing and sealing.

Strong light, especially sunlight, or wetting and drying repeatedly causes many fabrics to fade. The original sparkle and brilliance of the colors diminish and a once lively design becomes drab and tired looking. Quilts will fade under ordinary lights— incandescent and florescent. The best way to avoid this problem is to avoid displaying the fabrics under direct lighting. If you do want to show a special quilt as a wall hanging under a light or as a tapestry, rotate the fabric, if possible, so the color will fade evenly.

Light-fading isn't the only problem brought on by electric lights; heat damage is sometimes worse. The heat from an electric bulb has a weakening effect on the threads that hold the patchwork of a quilt. Old thread is sometimes so brittle that heat will crumble the threads without anyone or anything touching the quilt. And the fabric seems to mysteriously disintegrate. The solution is simple: turn off the lights when the quilt is not in view. Don't leave a quilt folded on the top of a heater or radiator.

Cleaning an Antique Quilt. After you have examined your quilt, aired it, rid it of unwanted insects or fungus, and shaken it free of foreign matter you are ready to really clean the quilt so it can be used for comfort, warmth, and to cover a baby or doll. Many people like to mend quilts before they are cleaned. This is done on the theory that when the quilt is cleaned the mending will be less noticeable. Others prefer to clean the quilt before mending, and if necessary, reclean. That seems a good system, although there is more mending to be done after most washings since they do subject the fabric to wear and tear.

The least offensive to most fabrics is washing in cool water. Least damaging is handwashing. Use a large basin or bathtub and submerge the quilt, including fabric layers and stuffing, under about two inches of soapy water. Use a mild soap or washing solution such as Woolite and squeeze the soapy water through the fabric. Do not wring or twist the quilt at any time. The water will probably be very muddy and several soapings necessary. The rinse should be very careful; run cool water through the fabric until it is free of fabric colorants or washing scum.

Almost as important as careful washing is drying and blocking the quilted fabric. After squeezing as much water from the fabric as possible spread the quilt flat on toweling and roll it jelly-roll style, and squeeze. This rids the quilt of most of the drippy moisture and also absorbs any color that might run. Keep the quilt flat. Do not hang any quilt from the corners or use clothespins letting the weight of the water-drenched fabric hang between the pins. You'll end up with a lumpy quilt. Allow the fabric to dry flat, placing it on a clean grassy lawn is best. In an apartment, place it over wooden bars or the shower stall.

As the fabric dries pull the corners firmly to form the original square or rectangle. Pat and press, urging the fabric into the original shape. Allow the quilt to dry until moist but not completely dry.

When moist and pliable, stretch the fabric again, this time pressing as you go. Use a medium warm iron and place the iron down on the fabric and then pick it up again rather than attempting to slide it along the patchwork. Use a pressing cloth if you find it convenient. As most quilts that are handmade have a variety of fabrics pressing must be guided by the fabric that requires the least heat—probably silk. Do not press a quilt as you would a garment. The iron is used to block and shape the quilt and revitalize the fibers.

The next step in refurbishing your quilt will be to seam, mend, tack, and restuff and retack the layers of fabric so that the quilt is as close as possible to the original. To do this you'll probably need the same quilting equipment mentioned on page 77. Add an embroidery needle with a large eye, several pairs of small sharp shears, and an embroidery hoop or small quilting frame.

Examine all the seams. If the quilt is composed of a front and back with stuffing or layered material within, it is best to find a weak seam on the outer edge and carefully open it so that the work can be done from the inside. If the quilt is in very poor condition opening a seam probably will not be necessary. Try to reconstitute the original seam and construction whenever possible.

Frayed material must be darned and mended, and patches can be inserted in the quilt pieces. Try not to replace quilt pieces, it is very difficult to find the right color and fabric—aged correctly—and it does more damage to the quilt as a collector's piece than a good job of careful mending. The detailed technique of mending can be found in US government booklets from the Department of Agriculture. The bibliography suggests some mending books. When the quilt is repaired you should keep in mind the following advice:

Do not clip or pierce the fabric in any way.

Avoid any uneven stress or strain on any part of the quilt.

Wash stains or spills as soon as possible.

Never use gummed tapes, rubber cement, iron-on patches, or any other bonding material on a quilt. The entire beauty of a quilt is its flexibility and texture.

Other Uses for Baby and Doll Quilts. While quilts are useful, attractive and serviceable as coverings they can be used in a variety of ways and for many purposes. Heavy quilts—those made from heavy fabric or using a heavy backing fabric—can be used for small rugs. They are particularly nice in front of a bed or as a play-mat for toddlers. Quilts are often used by hikers and campers because they are warm and snug and lightweight.

Although quilts, like any other fabric, can be used for many purposes the following ideas can be adapted for specific use with small quilts:

A card table cover.

A table or chair doily.

A stole or light poncho covering.

An apron.

Framed as a picture.

Small quilts and pieces of quilt can be used as chair seats, bags, cases, and shoulder straps for cameras or musical instruments.

However, remember that a baby quilt has its highest value when used for its original purpose, covering a sleeping baby.

Storing a Quilt. There are times when you cannot display your quilt and you want to store it. To keep your quilt in the best condition it is good to follow these suggestions:

Never store a soiled, stained or dirty quilt.

Never store a moist or damp quilt.

Before storing clean and mend your quilt.

Wrap your quilt in plain white tissue paper or brown wrapping paper before storing; never use newspaper.

Keep the quilt in a dry cool place if possible.

Roll the quilt and keep in a plastic bag if you have limited space.

Many people use moth-balls or spray garments and bedding with insect repellants before storing, but since the long-term effects of that practice are not known it might be best to keep the quilt as clean and dry as possible, and not add any other elements.

Displaying an Antique Quilt. Beauty and craft are meant to be admired. Display your treasured quilt whenever possible. One quilt, displayed as a tapestry over a sofa or as the central focal point in a modern room is dramatic. Several quilts can be mounted and displayed as a color panel on a door or on a folding screen. Several kinds of patterns and a variety of colors can be unified by mounting them all on the same solid color background.

A quilt collection is a source of great joy and can be an important and valuable investment. As in any antique object, the supply is limited and the demand is constantly growing. If you do have a collection, you may mount your quilts in safety and full view by having them framed much as one would valuable pictures. Plastic screen panels allow you to place quilts on both sides of the panel—to store and display them at the same time. It is most attractive to display quilts in their natural setting: what could be more charming than a cradle that contained a collection of quilts. Show and display your quilts to share the beauty and skill that is part of their heritage.

62. DOLL QUILT
   c. 1890
   11½″ × 11½″
   Four gold diamonds form center motif with red floral cutouts
   appliquéd on midnight blue background with striped blue border.
   Collection of Richard and Rosemarie Machmer

63. LADY OF THE LAKE
c. 1885
33″ × 38½″
Pieced cotton. Six groupings of red-black and white-black cotton triangles, set in wild geese borders.
Collection of Chase Manhattan Bank

64. HEARTS AND GIZZARDS
c. 1880
Massachusetts
34″ × 38″
Pink and white pieced cotton hearts, alternating with triangular
shapes form all-over pattern.
Collection of Phyllis Haders

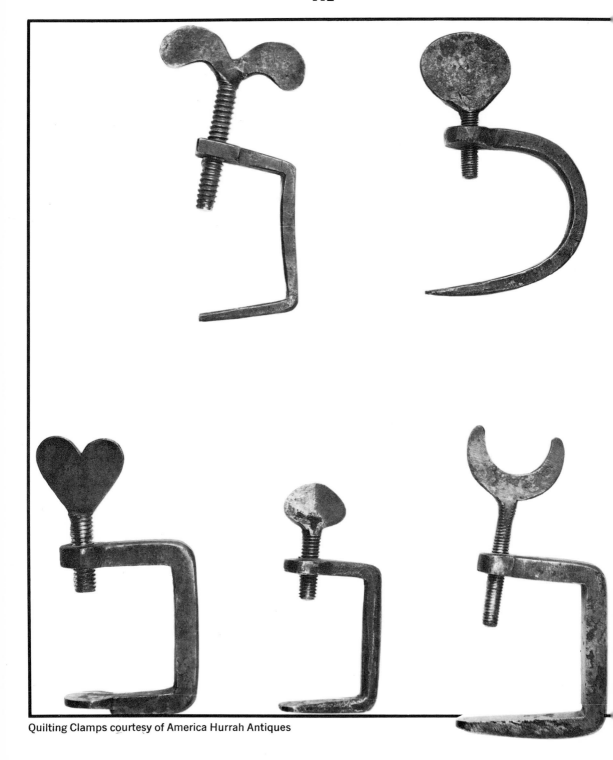

Quilting Clamps courtesy of America Hurrah Antiques

GLOSSARY

A List of Quilting Terms Used in this Book

Appliqué: The applying of one piece of fabric onto another and the securing of the top piece by stitching. An appliqué design is usually made up of many pieces laid on a solid piece of fabric and stitched into place.

Backing: The bottom layer of a quilt. The backing is usually cut from a solid or printed fabric and measures, in most cases, the same dimensions as the quilt top.

Bias Strips: Made by folding a diagonal line across the weave of the fabric. When 1½"-strips of fabric are cut on the bias, they can be used to finish off the quilt's raw outer edges.

Binding Off: Finishing off the raw outer edges of a quilt.

Block: A unit of patchwork usually designed within a square or other rectangle. These units, joined together, form a quilt top.

Crazy Quilt: The showcase for stitching skills and fabric collections. Often the crazy quilt was made from irregular pieces of silks, satins, velvets and brocades. These pieces were laid out on a muslin in a random design, turned under ¼" and stitched into place. Then the most beautiful and elaborate stitchery was used along the outer edges of each piece as a finishing touch. The Victorian era was the heyday of the crazy quilt; it was used as a decorative object adorning the piano, draped over a table or thrown over the arm of a chair.

Hexagonal Quilt: A pieced quilt made up completely of hexagons. Optical effects are produced by the contrast between light and dark tonal qualities.

Log Cabin Quilt: A type of quilt made entirely of blocks, each one composed of a center square with narrow rectangular pieces surrounding it. A contrasting effect is achieved between the lighter and darker tonal qualities by the way in which the individual blocks are set.

Piecing: Joining one piece of fabric to another by pinning, sewing and pressing.

Quilt: A bed cover consisting of three layers—top, stuffing and backing.

Quilting: Securing the layers of a quilt together with the running stitch.

Running Stitch: The most popular stitch in quilting. The needle is inserted through all the layers of the quilt, passing in and out several times before it is pulled through. Care should be taken to make the stitches as neat, tiny and uniform as possible (using your thimble, of course).

Setting: The joining together of finished blocks to produce a pleasing effect.

Stuffing (also called **batting**): A Dacron or cotton fiber filler placed between the top and backing to give a quilt more body and warmth.

Template: A full-scale cardboard pattern.

Trapunto (from the Italian word meaning "embroidered"): Sometimes called "Italian quilting," a technique of quilting done in double rows to delineate a pattern, forming an area into which cotton is stuffed from the back to create a raised effect.

Tufting: A stitch made at intervals and tied through all layers of a quilt in order to hold them together.

Whitework: A quilt made of two sheets of white fabric with thin interlining as the stuffing. The white quilting is worked throughout to produce a decorative and ornate design.

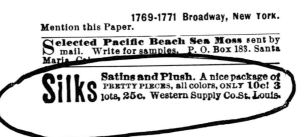

BOOKS ABOUT QUILTING

The following list does not include all excellent books on the subject of quilting. This is because there are just too many—quilting is very popular —and while the books included are all addressed to quilters who are making adult quilts, the same techniques are suitable for the smaller-scale coverlets.

Bacon, Lenice Ingram. AMERICAN PATCHWORK QUILTS. William Morrow and Company, New York, 1973. 192 pages. Illustrated, color pictures, bibliography, and index. $16.50.

Carlisle, Lilian Baker. PIECED WORK AND APPLIQUÉ QUILTS AT SHELBURNE MUSEUM. Hobby House Press, Maryland, 1967. 112 pages. Illustrated, paperback edition. $4.50.

Colby, Averil. QUILTING. Charles Scribner's Sons, New York, 1971. 212 pages. Illustrated with photographs, bibliography, and index. $12.50.

Foote, Estelle. THE MENDER'S MANUAL: *Repairing and Preserving Garments and Bedding.* Harcourt Brace Jovanovich, New York, 1976. 192 pages. Illustrated. $5.95.

Gutcheon, Beth. THE PERFECT PATCHWORK PRIMER. David McKay Company, New York, 1973. 226 pages. Illustrated, suppliers' lists, index. $9.95.

Ickis, Margurite. THE STANDARD BOOK OF QUILTING AND COLLECTING. Dover Publications, New York, 1949. 276 pages. Illustrations, index. $3.00.

Lewis, A. A. THE MOUNTAIN ARTISANS QUILTING BOOK. Macmillan, New York, 1973. 176 pages. Illustrations, color photographs. 173.

McKim, Ruby Short. ONE HUNDRED AND ONE PATCHWORK PATTERNS, revised edition. Dover Publications, New York, 1962. 124 pages. Illustrations. $2.00.

Meyer, Carolyn. MISS PATCH'S LEARN-TO-SEW BOOK. Harcourt Brace Jovanovich, New York, 1967. 72 pages. Illustrated. $4.95.

Meyer, Carolyn. STITCH BY STITCH: *Needlework for Beginners.* Harcourt Brace Jovanovich, New York. 1970. 96 pages. Illustrated with line drawings. Suitable for children who want to start quilt-making. $5.50.

Short, Eirian. QUILTING. Charles Scribner's Sons, New York, 1974. 88 pages. Illustrated with black and white photographs, and color photographs, line drawings, and patterns. $7.95.

357B   A Stitch in time saves nine.

Courtesy of America Hurrah Antiques